The Second Epistle of Paul to Timothy

E. Seabrooks

Copyright 2017 by Edward L. Seabrooks.
The book author retains sole copyright to
his contributions to this book.
Published 2017.
Printed in the United States of America.

All rights reserved.

No portion of this book may be reproduced, stored in a retrieval system, or transmitted in any form or by any means – electronic, mechanical, photocopy, recording, scanning, or other – except for brief quotations in critical reviews or articles, without the prior written permission of the author.

ISBN 978-1-946234-06-3

Front cover design by Mark Gauthier.

This book was published by BookCrafters,
Parker, Colorado.
bookcrafterscolorado@gmail.com

This book may be ordered from
www.bookcrafters.net and other online bookstores.

Foreword

Thank you for selecting this volume of the Expository series. These volumes are the contribution of various Apostolic writers. Their biography is on the back cover. The publishers of the Expository series would like to extend a thank you for helping us get this valuable material into the hands of readers.

The desire is that people would read the scriptures and be blessed. These commentary works, or works of Expository subjects, will give insight to, and further the understanding of the readers.

Each of these authors hold the values of the original Apostles of Jesus Christ. These writers want to hold to the values expostulated in the New Testament by Jesus and his disciples. Each of them ascribe to the concept offered by the Apostle John, "I have no greater joy than to hear that my children walk in truth."

Truth has been passed down through generations and has survived critics and doubters. Truth will prevail and ultimately triumph.

These writings are our contribution to the river of written truth that has flowed down through the ages.

Read and be blessed.

Kenneth Bow

Author and Date

The issue of Paul's authorship of the Pastoral Epistles is discussed in the Introduction to I Timothy: Author and Date. Paul wrote II Timothy, the last of his inspired letters, shortly before his martyrdom (c. A.D. 67).

Background and Setting

Transported from Rome to Ephesus--Paul has again found himself in prison in Rome, apparently rearrested during Nero's persecutions of Christians. Unlike his certain hope of release obvious in the first epistle to Timothy, there is none of that in this second letter. Paul knows his time has come—he was under house arrest when he wrote the first epistle, but now he is in a cold, damp cell (4:13), in chains (2:9), with no expectation of release (4:6). Paul requested of Timothy to bring him a cloke and his books, but we do not know whether Timothy made it to Rome before Paul's execution. Thus, he passes the mantle of ministry to Timothy, exhorts him to faithfulness (1:6), to hold fast to sound doctrine (1:13, 14), avoid error (2:15-18), and put his trust in the Scriptures and preach them unremittingly (3:15; 4:5).

Historical and Theological Themes

It is possible that Paul may have had reason to fear that Timothy was in danger spiritual abating. Certainly this was a serious concern for Paul since Timothy was considered necessary to carry on Paul's efforts. This unease is apparent, for example, in Paul's exhortation to "stir up" his gift (1:6), to replace fear with power, love, and a sound mind (1:7), to not be ashamed of Paul and the Lord, but willingly suffer for the gospel (1:8), and to hold on to the truth (1:13, 14). Since Timothy was knowledgeable in Paul's theology, Paul did not instruct him further doctrinally. He did, however, allude to numerous significant doctrines, and wrote the critical text of the New Testament on the inspiration of Scripture (3:16, 17).

1.1-5 Paul, an apostle of Jesus Christ by the will of God, according to the promise of life which is in Christ Jesus, 2 To Timothy, my dearly beloved son: Grace, mercy, and peace, from God the Father and Christ Jesus our Lord. 3 I thank God, whom I serve from my forefathers with pure conscience, that without ceasing I have remembrance of thee in my prayers night and day; 4 Greatly desiring to see thee, being mindful of thy tears, that I may be filled with joy; 5 When I call

to remembrance the unfeigned faith that is in thee, which dwelt first in thy grandmother Lois, and thy mother Eunice; and I am persuaded that in thee also.

1.1-5 An apostle. [one sent with a commission] **of Jesus Christ** (lit., "from Jesus Christ"). The formality of the initial verses indicate that the letter was perhaps intended for a broader readership then the primary addressee (Timothy). **Forefathers.** Paul indicates to Timothy that there is "*nothing new under the sun*," but rather a fulfillment. Further, he is merely manifesting an understanding that Christianity was not a totally new religion, but the ongoing work of the one God. A divinely purposed sequel and fulfillment of Judaism. Paul had simply moved on within the revealed plan of God. He was confident in this position and had a clear conscience (II Cor. 1:12). **The unfeigned** (*anupokritos*) — *un-hypocritical; without disguise...* **faith that is in thee**. Unmistakably, Lois and Eunice, had followed this same example. They had learned the Holy Scriptures and drew on them for a steady faith. They taught the scriptures to Timothy and he also developed a love and understanding of them. When faith becomes a "hand-me-down" item from generation to generation, we end up with "cookie-cutter Pentecostals," who have but a "form" at best. Faith is not a genetic disposition, but rather "contagious" when our children and others see it lived out. Heaven discriminates against grandchildren — only sons and daughters are allowed!

1.6-18 Wherefore I put thee in remembrance that thou stir up the gift of God, which is in thee by the putting on of my hands. 7 For God hath not given us the spirit of fear; but of power, and of love, and of a sound mind. 8 Be not thou therefore ashamed of the

testimony of our Lord, nor of me his prisoner: but be thou partaker of the afflictions of the gospel according to the power of God; 9 Who hath saved us, and called us with an holy calling, not according to our works, but according to his own purpose and grace, which was given us in Christ Jesus before the world began, 10 But is now made manifest by the appearing of our Saviour Jesus Christ, who hath abolished death, and hath brought life and immortality to light through the gospel: 11 Whereunto I am appointed a preacher, and an apostle, and a teacher of the Gentiles. 12 For the which cause I also suffer these things: nevertheless I am not ashamed: for I know whom I have believed, and am persuaded that he is able to keep that which I have committed unto him against that day. 13 Hold fast the form of sound words, which thou hast heard of me, in faith and love which is in Christ Jesus. 14 That good thing which was committed unto thee keep by the Holy Ghost which dwelleth in us. 15 This thou knowest, that all they which are in Asia be turned away from me; of whom are Phygellus and Hermogenes. 16 The Lord give mercy unto the house of Onesiphorus; for he oft refreshed me, and was not ashamed of my chain: 17 But, when he was in Rome, he sought me out very diligently, and found me. 18 The Lord grant unto him that he may find mercy of the Lord in that day: and in how many things he ministered unto me at Ephesus, thou knowest very well.

1.6-18 **Stir up the gift** (*charisma*) — *a gift of grace, involving grace on the part of the donor*...**of God**. Stir up means literally "to keep the fire alive." Paul reminds Timothy that as a steward of his God-given gift for preaching, teaching, and evangelizing, he could not let it fall into neglect. **Laying on of my hands** — a distinctive Apostolic custom. **A spirit of fear**. The Greek word, which can also be translated "timidity", denotes a cowardly, shameful fear caused by a weak, selfish character. **Who hath saved us, and called [us] with an holy calling**. Grace is the act of God giving salvation as a free gift to one who does not only not deserve it, but who deserves punishment for his sins. Grace, however, does not release one from the responsibility to "*repent and believe the gospel*" (Mark 1:15). We must exercise faith, then obey the terms of the gospel. **Appointed a preacher** (*kerux*) — *a herald of divine truth...* **of the gospel. Hold fast to the form** (*hupotuposis*) — *a sketch for imitation; pattern*. If thirty-five percent of the pastoral epistles involves directives regarding counterfeit teachers, false doctrines, and keeping the faith, then we should not be hesitant as "herald's of truth," "preachers" to sound the alarm. In our day, sure it might provoke the lovers of liberalism to make accusations of: too issue oriented, divisive, and negative; but let the accusers rant and rave. When the dust of so called "relevance" settles, only those who have maintained "the form of sound words" will be able to say as Paul, "I have kept the faith." **They which are in Asia**. A Roman province that is part of Modern Turkey; this is not a reference to the entire region of Asia Minor. **Phygellus and Hermogenes**. Apparently these two men had shown promise as leaders, but ultimately deserted Paul under the pressure of persecution. **Onesiphorus**. By contrast, Onesiphorus is commended for rendering services of love to Paul after finding him in a Roman dungeon; for he was not ashamed of his bonds, and "refreshed" him often.

2.1-26 Thou therefore, my son, be strong in the grace that is in Christ Jesus. 2 And the things that thou hast

heard of me among many witnesses, the same commit thou to faithful men, who shall be able to teach others also. 3 Thou therefore endure hardness, as a good soldier of Jesus Christ. 4 No man that warreth entangleth himself with the affairs of this life; that he may please him who hath chosen him to be a soldier. 5 And if a man also strive for masteries, yet is he not crowned, except he strive lawfully. 6 The husbandman that laboureth must be first partaker of the fruits. 7 Consider what I say; and the Lord give thee understanding in all things. 8 Remember that Jesus Christ of the seed of David was raised from the dead according to my gospel: 9 Wherein I suffer trouble, as an evil doer, even unto bonds; but the word of God is not bound. 10 Therefore I endure all things for the elect's sakes, that they may also obtain the salvation which is in Christ Jesus with eternal glory. 11 It is a faithful saying: For if we be dead with him, we shall also live with him: 12 If we suffer, we shall also reign with him: if we deny him, he also will deny us: 13 If we believe not, yet he abideth faithful: he cannot deny himself. 14 Of these things put them in remembrance, charging them before the Lord that they strive not about words to no profit, but to the subverting of the hearers. 15 Study to shew thyself approved unto God, a workman that needeth not to be ashamed, rightly dividing the word of truth. 16 But shun profane and vain babblings: for they will increase unto more ungodliness. 17 And their word will eat as doth a canker: of whom is Hymenaeus and Philetus; 18 Who concerning the truth have erred, saying that the resurrection is past already; and overthrow the faith of some. 19 Nevertheless the foundation of God standeth sure, having this seal, The Lord knoweth them that are his. And, let every one that nameth the

name of Christ depart from iniquity. 20 But in a great house there are not only vessels of gold and of silver, but also of wood and of earth; and some to honour, and some to dishonour. 21 If a man therefore purge himself from these, he shall be a vessel unto honour, sanctified, and meet for the master's use, and prepared unto every good work. 22 Flee also youthful lusts: but follow righteousness, faith, charity, peace, with them that call on the Lord out of a pure heart. 23 But foolish and unlearned questions avoid, knowing that they do gender strifes. 24 And the servant of the Lord must not strive; but be gentle unto all men, apt to teach, patient, 25 In meekness instructing those that oppose themselves; if God peradventure will give them repentance to the acknowledging of the truth; 26 And that they may recover themselves out of the snare of the devil, who are taken captive by him at his will.

2.1-26 Paul warns Timothy of the difficulties of the ministry and urges him to **be strong**, in contrast to those who had previously abandoned him. Timothy was being charged by his mentor to take some very challenging actions and steps, but he was not to be alone in the mission. **The same commit thou to faithful men**. He was to entrust the things he had been taught by Paul to responsible men who would in turn instruct others. In this way he would develop his ministry. Spreading the responsibility spreads the effect—it also spreads the recognition. Unselfish and unthreatened leaders do this without feeling threatened because they realize that this is not merely the task of delegation, but the extension of opportunity to those who may even be more effective then themselves. **Endure hardness** (*kakopatheo*)—*to undergo difficulties; be afflicted; suffer trouble.* **A good soldier**. The metaphor of the Christian life as warfare against evil and Satan. **Entangleth himself**. Just as a soldier called to duty is disengaged from the ordinary affairs of civilian life, so also must the good soldier of Jesus Christ refuse to allow the things of the world to distract him (1 John 2:15-17). **Strive for masteries** — the athlete. The Greek verb (*athleo*) expresses the effort and determination needed to compete successfully. **The husbandman**. Hardworking is from the Greek verb meaning "to labor to the point of exhaustion." Paul is urging Timothy not to be lazy or apathetic, but to labor intensely with a vision of the harvest. **Put them in remembrance** — means to remind them of these truths. **Subverting** (*Katastrophe*) — *an overthrow or overturn; figuratively, apostasy*. **Study** (*spoudazo*) — *to make a prompt effort; to give diligence*. **Rightly dividing** (*orthotomeo*) — *making a straight cut*. Exactitude and accuracy are key essentials in sound biblical interpretation, beyond all other enterprises, because the interpreter is handling God's Word. Flawed and distorted hermeneutics is usually the result of building a case for personal agendas. Make it plain. Cut it straight. Add nothing. Delete nothing. It's simple — just preach, teach, and live out unadulterated Truth! Ignoring to do so results in a (**canker**) gangrenous ulcer — a slow but sure dreadful fate. False teachers will come and go, but the "**foundation of God standeth sure**." They will certainly pass off the scene, but the church will stand triumphant. **The Lord knoweth them that are his**. For they are indeed **vessel**(s) **unto honor** and not dishonor — they have kept themselves unspotted by the world (James 1:27). They are **purge**(d) (*ekkathairo*) — *cleansed* and **sanctified** (*haziazo*) — *made holy, consecrated*. Resist **youthful lusts** that are deep seated desires which are particularly perilous to those who are young and unproven. But **follow** [lit., "pursue with intensity"] **righteousness**, those things that are consistent with the character of God. Thus leading to **repentance** (*metanoia*) — *a change of mind*.

3.1-17 This know also, that in the last days perilous times shall come. 2 For men shall be lovers of their own selves, covetous, boasters, proud, blasphemers, disobedient to parents, unthankful, unholy, 3 Without natural affection, trucebreakers, false accusers, incontinent, fierce, despisers of those that are good, 4 Traitors, heady, highminded, lovers of pleasures more than lovers of God; 5 Having a form of godliness, but denying the power thereof: from such turn away. 6 For of this sort are they which creep into houses, and lead captive silly women laden with sins, led away with divers lusts, 7 Ever learning, and never able to come to the knowledge of the truth. 8 Now as Jannes and Jambres withstood Moses, so do these also resist the truth: men of corrupt minds, reprobate concerning the faith. 9 But they shall proceed no further: for their folly shall be manifest unto all men, as their's also was. 10 But thou hast fully known my doctrine, manner of life, purpose, faith, longsuffering, charity, patience, 11 Persecutions, afflictions, which came unto me at Antioch, at Iconium, at Lystra; what persecutions I endured: but out of them all the Lord delivered me. 12 Yea, and all that will live godly in Christ Jesus shall suffer persecution. 13 But evil men and seducers shall wax worse and worse, deceiving, and being deceived. 14 But continue thou in the things which thou hast learned and hast been assured of, knowing of whom thou hast learned them; 15 And that from a child thou hast known the holy scriptures, which are able to make thee wise unto salvation through faith which is in Christ Jesus. 16 All scripture is given by inspiration

of God, and is profitable for doctrine, for reproof, for correction, for instruction in righteousness: 17 That the man of God may be perfect, thoroughly furnished unto all good works.

3.1-17 **The last days.** This phrase refers to this age, the time since the first coming of the Lord Jesus. **Perilous times** (*chalepos*) — *literally, hard times; grievous difficult.* Perilous times further indicate the apostasy that will take up residence in the finals days of the church age. **Lovers of their own selves** (*philautos*) — *of phileo, to be fond of and autos, self, i.e. fond of self.* **Lovers of pleasures**, points to a self first attitude. If pleasure and self-gratification are first, Jesus is not. **Having a form of godliness but denying the power thereof**. Form refers to the outward shape and appearance. **Power** (*dunamis*) — *power in the sense of that which overcomes resistance.* **Silly women** or gullible women are weak in virtue and knowledge of the truth, and weighed down with emotional and spiritual guilt over their sins, these women were easy prey for the deceitful, false teachers. **Ever learning, and never able to come to the knowledge of the truth** denotes some ambiguous quest for truth apart from God's word. **Jannes and Jambres**, according to Jewish custom were the two Egyptian magicians who tried at best to duplicate Moses' miracles. When it seems that there are more reprobates plying their deceit than there are truth declarers, remember that as Moses discomfited those ancient imposters, God will do so with modern deceivers. For "**they shall proceed no further: for their folly shall be manifest unto all [men], as theirs also was.**" **Thou hast fully known** (*parakoloutheo*) — *to follow after, as to always be at one's side, to conform to a pattern.* Timothy is given the inspiring example of Paul, and is reminded that he has, in the sacred Scriptures, a safeguard against all the influences of unsound doctrine. **Persecutions** and **afflictions** may take many forms and assume different levels of intensity, and as individuals we may not actually suffer physically as a result of the gospel. We all, however, have the devil to fight, the flesh to subdue, and our own carnality to deal with. **Continue** literally means "remain." **All Scripture is given by inspiration** (*theopneustos*) — *God breathed*. **Profitable for doctrine** or the source of doctrine — not subjective logic, not philosophy, not dreams, not spiritual euphoric experiences, not even heavenly visitations. The only reliable source of doctrine is the Bible. If doctrine cannot be found clearly stated in the Bible it should not be taught as authoritative. **Reproof — correction — instruction in righteousness** are permissible uses of the Word of God. This is God's design to straighten out our warped lives, thus aligning them to God's plan; to be **thoroughly furnished unto all good works**.

4.1-22 I charge thee therefore before God, and the Lord Jesus Christ, who shall judge the quick and the dead at his appearing and his kingdom; 2 Preach the word; be instant in season, out of season; reprove, rebuke, exhort with all long suffering and doctrine. 3 For the time will come when they will not endure sound doctrine; but after their own lusts shall they heap to themselves teachers, having itching ears; 4 And they shall turn away their ears from the truth, and shall be turned unto fables. 5 But watch thou in all things, endure afflictions, do the work of an evangelist, make full proof of thy ministry. 6 For I am now ready to be offered, and the time of my departure is at hand. 7 I have fought a good fight, I have finished my course, I have kept the faith: 8 Henceforth there is laid up

for me a crown of righteousness, which the Lord, the righteous judge, shall give me at that day: and not to me only, but unto all them also that love his appearing. 9 Do thy diligence to come shortly unto me: 10 For Demas hath forsaken me, having loved this present world, and is departed unto Thessalonica; Crescens to Galatia, Titus unto Dalmatia. 11 Only Luke is with me. Take Mark, and bring him with thee: for he is profitable to me for the ministry. 12 And Tychicus have I sent to Ephesus. 13 The cloke that I left at Troas with Carpus, when thou comest, bring with thee, and the books, but especially the parchments. 14 Alexander the coppersmith did me much evil: the Lord reward him according to his works: 15 Of whom be thou ware also: for he hath greatly withstood our words. 16 At my first answer no man stood with me, but all men forsook me: I pray God that it may not be laid to their charge. 17 Notwithstanding the Lord stood with me, and strengthened me; that by me the preaching might be fully known, and that all the Gentiles might hear: and I was delivered out of the mouth of the lion. 18 And the Lord shall deliver me from every evil work, and will preserve me unto his heavenly kingdom: to whom be glory for ever and ever. Amen. 19 Salute Prisca and Aquila, and the household of Onesiphorus. 20 Erastus abode at Corinth: but Trophimus have I left at Miletum sick. 21 Do thy diligence to come before winter. Eubulus greeteth thee, and Pudens, and Linus, and Claudia, and all the brethren. 22 The Lord Jesus Christ be with thy spirit. Grace be with you. Amen.

4.1-22 **I charge** (*diamarturomai*)—*a call to heaven and earth to witness what is about to be said*. Preach the word. Therein lies the duty of the ministry and the mantle of ordination— preach the word! **Be instant** (*epistemi*)—

to stand by, at hand, to be ready. **In season** (*eukairos*) — *opportune*. For the day has arrived when false **teachers** appeal to **itching ears** (*knethomenoi ton akoen*) — *hearing for mere gratification; salving the conscience.* Preacher don't accommodate the new worldly indulgences; rather, preach that which is not convenient. Strong preaching. Traditional preaching. Conservative preaching. We desire the "old paths!" **I have fought a good fight**. His approaching death is clearly on the Apostle's mind. **I have kept the faith**. The deposit of truth entrusted to him had been kept safe. Paul makes three personal requests of Timothy; **come shortly, take Mark, the cloke, the books, the parchments, bring with thee**. Is it not inspiring that the elder did not allow the weight of matters at the end of his life change his consecrated way of life? What a man loves most he would like to have near him in his last days. **The Lord stood with me** — the Lord fulfills His promise never to "leave or forsake" us. To underscore his altruistic mindset, Paul ends his letter with expressions toward and from his co-laborers in Christ. In the end he turns again to Timothy: "**The Lord Jesus Christ [be] with thy spirit. Grace [be] with you.**"

www.ingramcontent.com/pod-product-compliance
Lightning Source LLC
Chambersburg PA
CBHW040418100526
44588CB00022B/2874